SHE

SHE

An Expose' of Her Insufficiencies

M. DARLENE CARSON

J Merrill Publishing, Inc., Columbus 43207
www.JMerrill.pub

Copyright © 2021 J Merrill Publishing, Inc.
All rights reserved. No part of this publication may be reproduced, distributed, or transmitted in any form or by any means, including photocopying, recording, or other electronic or mechanical methods, without the prior written permission of the publisher, except in the case of brief quotations embodied in critical reviews and certain other noncommercial uses permitted by copyright law. For permission requests, contact J Merrill Publishing, Inc., 434 Hillpine Drive, Columbus, OH 43207
Published 2021

Library of Congress Control Number: 2021901995
ISBN-13: 978-1-950719-90-7 (Paperback)
ISBN-13: 978-1-950719-89-1 (eBook)

Title: SHE: An Expose' of Her Insufficiencies
Author: M. Darlene Carson
Editor: Dennis Brown
She Logo: Adam Dabilis
Cover Artwork: DPI Graphics, Derek Payne

To all of the strong, passionate, driven women who live their lives to the fullest and inspire others along the way.

Special Thanks

My Forever, Darrell Carson

Angela Cornelius Dawson

Shanikka Flinn

Lyn Hang

My Children

CONTENTS

Foreword	ix
Introduction	xiii
Preface	xix
SHE Strives toward the Ten Virtues of the Proverbs Woman	1
The Other Woman	5
Hustle and Wait	9
True Love	17
Cup of Joe	23
Aging Grace	29
His Heart	37
Perfect	45
Fixed	61
Weight on the Lord	67
Afterword	73
About the Author	77

FOREWORD

SHE is amazing.

I am speaking of both this book and the author, M. Darlene Carson. I have known her for over fifteen years. We worked together in a community-based treatment and prevention services agency. This provided me the opportunity to have a front-row seat to her creativity. Whether through stage play, poetry, or the prophetic word, Darlene can be relied upon to "keep it relevant."

Drawing from the well of her life experiences, Darlene is not afraid to go deep to provide a cool drink of relief for others.

She is always on the cutting edge of the issues that affect our community. She has never played it safe

FOREWORD

with cookie-cutter messages and fairy tale endings. Throughout all of her artistic endeavors, she has challenged her audiences to face the harsh realities of addiction, failed relationships, poor health, and family dysfunction within the backdrop of human struggles with a message to be hopeful, tenacious, and maintain our faith.

Her consistent down to earth approach allows the reader to gain insight into this expose' of insufficiencies portrayed so well that she will have you wondering which "SHE" you are.

Today we live in the age of Facebook, Twitter, and Instagram. We rarely take the time to reflect on our lives because we are always Linked In to "minding someone else's business."

This book provides the opportunity for us to spend some much-needed time logged into ourselves and focused on our own issues.

SHE is a must-read for sisters who need to be a friend to themselves and for brothers who are trying to understand the true profile of their woman. Book clubs should place this introspective read at the top of their list, as it will provide an excellent springboard to discuss our "SHE" issues.

This book is a timely unveiling of our tendency to act out on life's stage the unrealistic expectations

FOREWORD

downloaded into our scripts to be perfect. This revealing displays our ongoing struggle in our various roles of daughters, sisters, women, girlfriends, wives, saints, and professionals to be flawless.

In *SHE*, Carson provides a much-needed mirror to reflect the need for acceptance, boundaries, and self-love that creates the balance that YOU, SHE, and I need.

- Angela Cornelius Dawson

Angela Cornelius Dawson is a State Agency Director addressing Minority Health and a former State Agency Director over an Addiction Services and Community Prevention and Treatment Center for 20 years

INTRODUCTION

> *"...God who gives life to the dead and calls those things which do not exist as though they did..."*
>
> — ROMANS 4:17

When I think of all the phenomenal women God has placed around me, I am in awe of how they remain humble and never see themselves as exceptional. These women who have given me guidance, confidence, and unconditional love are living examples of the Virtuous Woman.

I often ponder whether I can be a shining example of the Proverbs 31 woman. This sister has it all together, or does SHE? I believe that the scripture

INTRODUCTION

gives us a guide to becoming a model of grace like her.

Does this mean that if one does not consistently exhibit all the Proverbs 31 virtues, she is not a "virtuous" woman?

If we are honest with ourselves, our daily lives (in contrast to the litmus test of the Proverbs 31 virtues) fall short of this glorious standard, and often we are left feeling quite inadequate. I mean, really? Just today, I overslept, over-ate, forgot to pay the electric bill, consciously procrastinated getting a couple of projects completed, and guess what else? My credit is less than stellar!

Listen, I love being a woman! But excuse me, I'm telling you – sometimes a woman's life is a real beast to navigate! And not just because of physical pain and nauseous periods that come with it, or how inconvenient having breasts really is, or the disrespect of sexism, or the fact that our hormones regulate our mood swings. And then there's childbirth? Let's not even talk about that!

This Proverbs 31 super *sistah* could not possibly have gone through all this, and she surely cannot exist in today's modern culture, or could she? I mean, she sounds much like the Enjoli woman (do you remember her?) she'll "...bring home the

INTRODUCTION

bacon, fry it up in the pan, and she never lets him forget he's a man!" She gets up super early, eats right, takes care of her husband, the kids, the homeless, and everybody else! It is no wonder she is worth far more than jewels. She's doing the work of a ton of people!

But let's admit the culture and customs in society today are greatly different from the Ancient near East and Greco-Roman world of Old and New Testament times. Let us consider that the Proverbs 31 woman lived in a man's world and had a "harder hill to climb." There were clearly strictly maintained gender roles and the culturally defined and defended emphasis on women's subservience. That alone would have caused many of us (me) to fail the test.

Believe me. I am not hyper-religious or self-righteous. In fact, I've fallen into my mess more times than I care to admit and have quite a long way to go to get to the Proverbs 31 woman God has shown me I can be. And what I love most about this journey of "becoming" is that we all can be unique versions of her. In a world filled with American idols, fake news, social chameleons, and superficialities, it is easy to feel like you have to fit into the world's ideal and definition of who you should be - not to mention the pressure that

INTRODUCTION

comes with facing your fears - of ultimately facing the "YOU" that only you know.

It is certainly easier to gravitate towards becoming the petty, vindictive, back-stabbing, money-grubbing, cliquish, disloyal, arrogant, self-involved, wasteful woman that the world shows on reality television than to be the woman of God described in Proverbs 31.

We are fearfully and wonderfully made (Psalm 139:15). We do not have to mimic someone else's style or the way that they act. Accept the fact that being YOU is amazing! You are an original. Your fingerprint is different, and you cannot be cloned, nor should you be.

Romans 12:1-2 tells us, "be ye transformed by the renewing of your mind." I believe that is one of the most important steps in truly becoming our best. We need to put off our own negative and corrupt thinking and put on God's thoughts to see ourselves as He sees us. Hush the murmurings whispered to you by the enemy! In your "becoming," understand that cynics who habitually express their pessimistic views about the vision of you and the dreams God has given you have no say in the matter. The word of God confirms that "the devil is a liar, " and you can believe the report of the Lord! One writer says, "The bigger God's opinion in your mind, the smaller the opinions of others."

Personally, some days I cannot see any parts of the virtuous woman within me. But I am learning to see myself through the eyes of the Creator. He uses His word and His principles to sculpt me into the woman He created me to be.

I am thankful that the strength girded in a woman's nature provides the ability to balance huge demands and others' pressures and expectations.

When we choose to model ourselves after this biblical example, we must learn to discipline our minds to focus on "becoming." It will not be an overnight transformation. In fact, we will never reach the Proverbs 31 perfection, but every step to become the woman God intended you to be will become a reality as long as you do not lose your stride.

As you read the introductory "Ten Virtues of the Proverbs Woman," rank yourself on a one-to-ten scale for each of those virtues that you exhibit consistently. Take heed in the reality that we will fall short in areas but relax and know that the grace of God provides a make-up test every day to get us where He desires us to be.

PREFACE

God has blessed me to have been raised by an amazing mother who was a spirit-filled example of strength despite life's circumstances. She overcame life challenges, and her work ethic and faith provided an example that guided me. However, I did not realize the value of her actions until I began to experience life as an adult.

From that point on, positioned at every place throughout my journey were strong, confident women who had their 'stuff' together. I saw that despite the pain and adversity that life dealt to them, they made decisions, took responsibility for their actions, faced challenges, and went through life with their heads held high.

PREFACE

SHE is a tribute to the strength of women everywhere and is meant to acknowledge their contributions and encourage them to embrace their strength, beauty, and the profound impact that they have on the world.

SHE STRIVES TOWARD THE TEN VIRTUES OF THE PROVERBS WOMAN

1. **FAITH** – SHE exhibits faith, putting trust in God alone and leaning not unto her own understanding. (Proverbs 31:26, Proverbs 31:29–31, Matthew 22:37, John 14:15, Psalm 119:15
2. **MARRIAGE** – SHE honors her husband and acts in his best interest. He can trust her as his helper. (Proverbs 31:11- 12, Proverbs 31:23, Proverbs 31:28, 1 Peter 3, Ephesians 5, Genesis2:18)
3. **MOTHERING** – SHE raises her children to serve God. SHE loves, nurtures, and disciplines them in the path of holiness so that they know righteousness. (Proverbs 31:28, Proverbs

31:26, Proverbs 22:6, Deuteronomy 6, Luke 18:16)

4. **HEALTH** – SHE takes care of herself – mind, soul and body and SHE is strengthened to take care of her family with provisions of food that is nourishing. (Proverbs 31:14–15, Proverbs 31:17, 1 Corinthians 6:19, Genesis 1:29, Daniel 1, Leviticus 11)

5. **SERVICE** – SHE serves and she gives with a positive and soft spirit (Proverbs 31:12, Proverbs 31:15, Proverbs 31:20, 1 Corinthians 13:13)

6. **FINANCES** – SHE is profitable in her work and is financially wise. SHE is a good example of stewardship. (Proverbs 31:14, Proverbs 31:16, Proverbs 31:18, 1 Timothy 6:10, Ephesians 5:23, Deuteronomy 14:22, Numbers 18:26)

7. **INDUSTRY** – SHE is a willing worker who uses her hands. SHE praises and worships God without complaint. (Proverbs 31:13, Proverbs 31:16, Proverbs 31:24, Proverbs 31:31, Philippians 2:14)

8. **HOMEMAKING** – SHE creates a home that is inviting, peaceful and filled with love for her family, friends and guests. (Proverbs 31:15, Proverbs 31:20–22,

Proverbs 31:27, Titus 2:5, 1 Peter 4:9, Hebrews 13:2)

9. **TIME** – SHE uses her time wisely and is diligent to set her hands to do those things that are right in the sight of God. (Proverbs 31:13, Proverbs 31:19, Proverbs 31:27, Ecclesiastes 3, Proverbs 16:9, Philippians 4:8)

10. **BEAUTY** – SHE has inner beauty and outer beauty. SHE is adorned in righteousness. SHE skillfully plans creatively for her family and edifies with her words. (Proverbs 31:10, Proverbs 31:21-22, Proverbs 31:24-25, Isaiah 61:10, 1 Peter 3:1-6)

THE OTHER WOMAN

"But you are to hold fast to the Lord your God, as you have until now."

— JOSHUA 23:8

Odessa was a mess. She was overcome with the stressors of life – pressured by the overload of her work mode and pimped out by everybody that needed something. They all seemed to know her better than she knew herself and took advantage of the fact that she could not say "no." She had a giving heart and went hard for everyone she loved. Self-care was not a priority for her, and she struggled with the reality of her health and age. Plus, she put everything into her marriage and was living through the painful experience of his infidelity. Enough was enough! That was the proverbial straw that broke the camel's back! When did this become her life?

It was an unrecognizable plethora of dysfunction and unhappiness! It looked nothing like her dreams, it did not reflect her vision board, and for all the prayers and tears she pushed through and sent up, apparently God had deserted her because her faith was weak and wavering.

Whatever the case, she sat there staring upward, giving God the stank-eye because she blamed Him, but in her heart of hearts, she held the faint knowledge that she did not want to accept that it was her own fault. For the ten plus years of their marital bliss, she had balanced her whole life – everything, every part of it - on her marriage, not realizing that God is the only one who is capable of being "her everything."

Her fantasies of their fairy tale love were destroyed and replaced with the grim reality and disappointment that she had been horribly deceived. Now here she was, months later, staring down into a cup of tea hosting her own pity party, mulling it over and trying to convince herself that this couldn't be happening. "NO, NO, NO! Not me, not him, not our marriage. He would not do this to me!" As she worked through the anger and grief, she told herself, "You are stupid! How could you not have known?"

No amount of self-talk made a difference. Moments later, there she was - laid out on the bathroom floor, crouched in a fetal position, tears streaming down her face. Over and over, she asked the million-dollar question, "How do I get over this?"

She managed to pull herself together, get up, and as she looked into the mirror – she told herself, "this is not the solution."

She took inventory of her life choices, her strengths and weaknesses. It forced her to recognize how she had sacrificed who she was, her own needs, and had stopped showing up in her own life to become what she thought he needed and to maintain what she thought their marriage needed. As she stared at her reflection, she noticed how much her physical appearance mirrored how she felt internally. Over time the stress had wreaked havoc on her natural beauty. The discrepancy between who she was when they met and who she had become was quite significant.

Then utter brilliance! She knew what she needed to do to get over it. She decided that she would introduce herself to the other woman, the one who was partially responsible for destroying what she had believed to be her "happily ever after." She imagined what this mystery woman would be like – beautiful, strong, and confident, with a mad hustle and a dope soul.

She finally met her and realized that she had known her all along. She lost touch with her over the years. Surprisingly, the woman took responsibility for the role she played in her own life's fiasco.

Odessa decided at that very moment to stop feeling sorry for herself. She looked again into the mirror and validated her own beauty with a thankful heart and said hello and welcome back to her long-lost self. She vowed within that moment that she would never close her eyes to her true self ever again and would always hold on to God tighter than she could ever hold on to a man.

HUSTLE AND WAIT

"Therefore, return to your God, observe kindness and justice, and wait for your God continually."

— *HOSEA 12:6*

Wiping the tears from her eyes, Imani attempted to get off her knees. But each time, she sensed the supernatural presence of God more strongly, and a soul praise would shutter through the depths of her belly giving place to inaudible rejoicing and quickening within her spirit. Finally, able to bring herself more or less under control, she got up feeling relieved and lifted but made the mistake of looking over to her desk at the looming pile of debts that jerked her back to a harsh reality and hampered the peace of mind she had just found. The joyous release that blessed her was yet again overcome by exhaustion and exasperation.

She sat down at her desk and grabbed the pile of waiting bills, "God, when will you help me" she growled, frustratedly tossing them in the air. The papers flew everywhere - across the desk, into her lap, and onto the floor. She immediately felt terribly ashamed for taking her failings out on God. She shook her head and smiled with a wry twist of her mouth and bent down to pick up the paper-strewn evidence of her tantrum while subconsciously thinking to herself that it would take a forty-day fast, sackcloth, ashes, and a literal act of God to deliver her from the predicament she found herself in.

Imani's worries had induced an ulcer due to money problems and financial troubles from a marriage that ended with racked up debt and ruined credit. She was now a part of the working poor, at risk of being homeless. Her depleted bank account, hand me down furniture, and thrift store clothes reflected zero luxuries. As a single mother of two, she was barely staying afloat. Her faith had grown very weak, but she tried to make up for it with her gratitude. She always acknowledged with thanksgiving the blessings that she knew had to come from God Himself.

She heard her cell phone ring and disregarded it, allowing the voicemail message to greet one of the many bill collectors that bombarded her daily. She endured threats of garnishment, car repossession, as well as the cutting off of her utilities. She had become a finagler, robbing Peter to pay Paul and the rest of Jesus' disciples.

In less than five minutes, the phone rang again and displayed an unidentified number. She answered with a reluctant, "This is Imani." It was a reminder call regarding her promise to pay on the quick cash loan due the next day. She engaged the curt collection agent with back-and-forth exchanges. Finally, she made a second arrangement, which she politely promised to pay. After hanging up, she frantically punched in numbers on her calculator, trying to find more money to cover her expenses miraculously. No matter how she added it up, it was never enough.

She inhaled heavily and blew out air slowly. Before she could take another breath, the phone rang again, but this time she recognized the number. She picked up, and before she could even speak, the voice on the other end of the phone said, "Hey,

Mani, I got 'that' if you still need it!" Her cousin Ellai had a little "food stamp hustle," and to feed her own children, Imani was always more than willing to take advantage of the opportunity to stretch her money and get twice the food for half the price. Imani gave a quick-fire response, "Not this time." The answer popped out of her mouth so fast that she startled herself. Bewildered by her own response, she found herself silently preoccupied with swirling ideas in her head of what she would do now that she had just passed on her usual hook-up.

Imani came from a hustle type environment, so hustle was a part of her DNA, just like her eye color. She figured out creative ways to get what she needed without being blatantly outside of the law. Her mind persuaded her that she had the right - or perhaps the duty - to disobey the law when the system's bureaucracy did not work for her. As hard as she worked for her money, she still lived at 20% below the federal poverty level. It was humiliating enough without the added indignity of reaching out for help and being treated like a Mercedes driving welfare queen living high on the hog on the backs of good old tax-paying citizens. It cooked her grits that the social system did not always work for those who needed help the most.

By now, Imani had zoned all the way out, knowing Ellai was saying something, yet not hearing a word. She nodded her head slightly as her cousin talked but was barely paying attention. "Girl, are you for sure? 'Cause I know you on a struggle right now and can't afford to get them all! So, how about this? I'll give you fifty for twenty-five. I need to move them right away; I've got some things to take care of. Come on and hook a sistah up."

"Nah, I'm good," Imani assured. Unable to persuade her cousin, Ellai angrily snapped back in a harsh, sarcastic tone. "A'ight then, when you through waitin' on Jesus, call me – I may have som'in left to keep my little cousins from starvin'!"

Hearing her ghetto mouthed close family member's smug words hurt like fire to flesh and infuriated Imani. But, she squeezed her eyes shut, bit her lip, and maintained her composure, "Ellai, you called me, so apparently, you need me more than I need you!"

She knew how ignorant and vindictive Ellai could be when someone shut her hustle down, so she hung up before they both said something that they would regret.

Lately, Imani's temper would rise at the slightest infraction like mercury in a thermometer next to a lit match, and it was with difficulty that she kept from reverting to her old nature. She was always careful to reflect to others the testimony of Christ in her life. Still, she privately found herself searching for what was left of the little faith she professed.

As she put her papers back on the desk, she tried not to let Ellai's words eat away at her spirit, yet she could not shake what she was feeling.

"The audacity of that swindling heifer. I don't need her help." She shrugged, gave a grim smile, drew her hands across her eyes as if to wipe away her worry. But quick flashbacks played in her head – everything from fleeing her abusive marriage, pawning her jewelry, and spending everything to provide for her children and pay her bills.

And just that quickly, God nudged Imani, reminding her of her complaint against Ellai, and the truth echoed deep within her. She had compromised God's word with her "hustle and wait" mindset. Whenever she found herself in fits of despair, she prayed and studied God's word but never took His promises literally. Instead, she gave in to the impulse to fight her own battles. Weary of waiting on God, she devised plans that went against what she claimed to believe. Her prayers were hollow cries that told God the same thing she told her cousin, "I don't need your help." As she inventoried all the times when she had "helped God" and thought things had turned out alright, she realized that she came up short. The calculation: zero.

At that moment, she felt a peace wash over her and arrest her wrong head notions and hustling heart. She immediately repented, decided then and there to place herself in a position to hear from the Spirit and receive His help. Feeling stiff from sitting so long, she got up from her rickety chair and put the stack of bills away. Taking a seldom-used position, she bent down to her knees to pray, knowing this, God had been faithful in the past, and she was sure He would be faithful again.

TRUE LOVE

"Blessed is she who has believed that the Lord would fulfill His promises to her!"

— LUKE 1:45

In the full throes of feeling sorry for herself, Kendall wrapped up in the warmth of her favorite chenille throw and made herself comfortable on the large red microfiber sofa. She was always cold. Being diagnosed anemic as a child, she knew that binging on Haagen-Dazs chocolate chip ice cream would make her shiver until her teeth chattered. But the rich flavor and deliciousness of the experience was worth the chill. Believing that her mind-numbing misery was worthy of documentation, she grabbed her iPhone, snapped photos of her current situation – ice cream, Netflix, and Kleenex - and posted them to her social media networks with the caption: "Pity Party Supplies. #Rain"

A popular bible toting, scripture quoting Christian lifestyle blogger, Kendall had over four thousand followers on Twitter, Facebook, and Snapchat. The crux of her popularity was due to her non-preachy, transparent humanness. Although she was great at encouraging her readers to navigate through the stuff of life, she didn't have the strength to encourage herself in her own situation.

Her virtual communities responded with a ton of positive responses. She was slapped in the face equally with a slew of negative comments. Kendall ignored her cyber-bullies with silence, but she sometimes internalized their criticisms furthering the personal angst that she lived every day as her own worst critic.

She tried watching her favorite love stories on Netflix. But turned it off because her present worries absorbed every faculty of her mind. As the hours ticked by, she wrestled with her stupidity at losing the love of her life. She fondly remembered how close they used to be, and her heart was sorry for not cherishing what they had. Moreover, she felt guilty for carelessly neglecting their relationship and for her unfaithfulness to the vow she made to him.

Furiously patting her head to relieve the itching of her fresh, tightly done shoulder-length Ghanaian braids, Kendall looked around and retrieved the fork she used to devour the Chicken Lo Mein and used it to get at the scalp beneath her braids. Sucking in her breath as she soothed her scalp, she lamented, "The price you pay for beauty!"

Out of nowhere, a random Ted Taylor song popped into her head, the same one that her mother played over and over again when Kendall was a child. "Only the lonely knows the joy of a knock on the door, a ring on the telephone so you know that you're not alone, only the lonely knows..."

"The devil is a liar!" she exclaimed. Her outburst was an indicator that any lyrics that suggested she should endure a life of loneliness were simply not welcome.

Kendall stretched her arms as far as she could, threw her face to the ceiling, and broke the silence with a loud and sleepy yawn. She brought her arms down in one smooth motion, reached for and ripped open a bag of kettle chips, threw a few in her mouth, and crunched loudly. As she savored the taste, she caught a glimpse of her reflection in the beveled wall mirror adjacent to the couch. She threw the bag down at the stark awareness that binging on crap food and feeling sorry for yourself would only make her sink deeper into her hopelessness.

This mess was her own fault. She readily took the blame. She emotionally abandoned him for distractions that were more interesting to her. At that moment, her thoughts went to the freedom and peace she felt when things were good between them. She smiled as her mind conjured up the memories of what they shared. He was such a gentleman. He gave her the freedom to chase her dreams, live her life with no strings. And eventually, he just let her be, not out of anger but out of his love for her.

She was so caught up in her own YOLO (You Only Live Once) lifestyle that she disregarded their relationship. After all, he said he would always be there, and she realized that she had taken advantage of that. When their love was new, they set-aside quiet, quality time together daily. After a while, though, she would end up on the computer or the phone or just doing her thing. In her own defense, she rationalized that there were many important things that she needed to do. Important in her own eyes, that is, but perhaps not from his point of view.

The love she was missing from him was no ordinary love. She had dated rascals, been engaged to a knucklehead, sent momma's boys back to their mommas, gotten tricked by gentlemen, and hit on by deacons, preachers, and bishops. Yet, she wanted the love that only he could provide. Kendall wondered, "How could I be so selfish?"

Deep inside, she could see her Nanna's tired yellow flecked eyes and hear her trembly voice, always fueled with concern and wisdom, coming back to bite her, "You don't miss your water until your well runs dry, baby!" She must've heard those words a thousand times. And they turned out to be profoundly prophetic because here she was fully living into it.

Her well was dry. Her soul was parched. Her heart was heavy and thirsting. She missed what they once had. Although she had not forgiven herself for the thoughtless behaviors that lead her to this place in her life, she craved his forgiveness. She wanted him so desperately that she constantly thought of begging for his return. Tears welled up in her eyes because she feared rejection at the thought of even asking.

She whispered to herself, practicing several different scenarios to approach him, "I was wrong, please forgive me." "I didn't mean to neglect you." "You see, what had happened was..." She laughed aloud at herself, "What's the use?" With so many others yearning for his attention, why would he even give me the time of day?

She shrugged and shook her head no. She had enough. The combination of tears and all the thoughts keeping her awake in the middle of the night was not helping her get him back. She needed to do something. She resolved to talk with him. She glanced at the clock and saw how late it was. But she set aside all of her troubling thoughts and followed her heart.

She set the atmosphere for their encounter. She turned the television off. She commanded Alexa to play the smooth jazz gospel of Kirk Whalum. She opened her heart to receive his presence. She closed her eyes, bowed her head, and called out to him. Tears of remorse fell like raindrops from her eyes; they rolled down her cheek and into her hands, "Jesus, I messed up, but forgive me." As simple as that, He welcomed her back, and she realized that His promise was true. He had been there all the time.

CUP OF JOE

"Weeping may endure for a night, but joy comes in the morning."

— PSALM 30:5

She loved coffee more than a crack fiend loved rock. A cup of fresh coffee was her 'got to have,' that morning hit of java that helped Juliana accept what the day would bring. Living with *him*, the day always delivered something that was totally jacked up.

She sat silently, half-way meditating and half-way letting the rich aroma of the brewed coffee take her to sweet memories of times past, a time when her life wasn't so complicated.

As she pondered her life's journey, she realized that she was a devoted slave to the teapot – ginger chai before Joseph. They met at a park, fell in lust disguised as love. They began meeting every morning at Starbucks.

She was smitten. Everything about him turned her on – his sense of humor and his style. She was clearly mesmerized by his charm. So much so, in fact, that she lost her sense of self. "Try new things, don't be trapped in a routine," he had admonished her.

And then, one day, she gave in to his suggestion. The barista prepared 'Bold Roast. Plain. Nothing in it.' based upon his recommendation. There, her coffee bias began. To her, the drink was now the nectar of life.

One day, as she sipped her coffee reflectively, Juliana became ruthlessly honest with herself. She nodded her head side to side in near disbelief that her one concession to trade her tea for coffee had led one by one to so many others, all so far more consequential that she hardly recognized the person she had become. She felt tossed in a sea of internal conflict between her heart and her head. She used to feel something special at the sight of him, but now she felt nothing.

His demanding and controlling attitude had crushed her once free spirit, and their six-year relationship felt more like a stint in prison with no parole. His overwhelming insecurities often played out in physical violence. There were the repeated black-eyes, bruises, busted lips, and contusions. He would routinely monitor her calls and even smell her to make sure she had not cheated on him. And the verbal abuse seemed to constantly get worse. She had grown weary of him punching walls and throwing objects at her. Julianna had become accustomed to blaming herself for his endless tirades and came to expect an altercation for any trivial reason he took a notion to. And in the back of her mind, she wondered if he would kill her one day.

Then came the day when she realized that his behavior outweighed the traits that had caused her to fall in love with him. It was that love that had caused her to ignore the monster he had become.

But not today. Today, her usual blend of coffee (or "bean juice," as she called it) seemed to awaken her, and each sip became a fresh surge of liquid courage.

The squeaky kitchen screen door opened, slammed shut, and startled her, intruding on her thoughts. She looked up into Joseph's face, and before she could even acknowledge his presence, he immediately went off on her about some random nonsense that she didn't want to hear. She slowly and deliberately stood to her feet, picked up her coffee mug, took a large swig, and proceeded to walk away in silence. But he positioned himself in front of her to block her way. "Where do you think you're going?" he said hatefully, snatching her so tightly by the arm that the pain was immediately overwhelming. The mug of sippable deliciousness fell to the ground, shattering and spilling onto the black and white checkered laminate floor tiles.

The fact that he put his hands on her again thoroughly pissed her off. What he didn't know was that Julianna was "coffee-drunk" by now, and seeing her rich, bold roast on the floor flipped a switch on. The caffeine had stirred her indignation and what emerged was a caf-fiend.

She drank at least a gallon of java a day. Her never-ending thirst for that jitter in a cup had her amped. Hopped up on caffeine and the anxiety that came from his actions, her adrenaline was revved up for a battle she refused to lose. "Let go of me, Joseph! You're hurting me!" she cried vehemently. Her heart raced as she furiously jerked away from his vice-like grip, causing him to lose his balance on the wet tiles. He went down in slow motion, hitting his head on the edge of the marble kitchen counter. Stunned, dazed, and confused, he tried to muster the wherewithal to get up. But, before he could, Julianna went berserk, punching him and kicking him several times in his groin. He screamed like a girl and moaned uncontrollably as he clutched his crotch in excruciating agony. "Okay! Stop! Stop!" Joseph lamented, struggling to articulate his plea. Without a word, she reached down and grabbed a handful of his shoulder-length brown locks, pulled his head up, and knee butted him in the face! He blurted out one final gasp, his head fell back, and he lay sprawled out on the floor, unconscious, bloody nosed, hurt pride and all.

A strong sense of sadistic satisfaction flowed through Julianna as she stood over him. She gazed first at his face and the rest of his body, mentally inventorying his injuries. Then she squatted at his side, took his wrist, and checked his pulse. Alive. She didn't want him dead. She just wanted to teach him a lesson. That was all.

Finally, the voices that had told her for so long to stay with him had been evicted.

Julianna pulled and tugged to adjust her clothes, finger fluffed her short curls, and checked her watch to confirm the time. Just in time, she thought. The automatic coffee maker had done its job. She headed toward the kitchen cabinet, retrieved her travel mug, and poured herself a fresh cup of Chai ginger tea. No more of the devil's brew. She was done with Joe.

With the packed bags she had kept in her car for quite a while, she was exhilarated to finally be free.

AGING GRACE

"Even to your old age and gray hairs, I am He who will sustain you. I have made you and I will carry you; I will sustain you and I will rescue you."

— ISAIAH 46:4

A tinge of warmth kissed her face as the bathing rays of sun came streaming down from the glass skylight above her queen-sized bed and lit the room. As she lay still drowsy, in her usual can't-get-out-of-bed stupor, the soft sound of her alarm clock went off as it did every day at precisely 8:00 a.m. It startled her into wakefulness.

Her first thought was to throw the wretched device as far away as possible so she could get back to sleep in peace, but instead, she reached out a hand and blindly turned off the alarm. As usual, her mind was immediately cluttered with the "to do" lists, tasks, and obligations that she needed to get done. But, like every morning, she gave in to the instinct to just lay there, indulging her laziness and tendency toward procrastination.

In her mid-50s, Grace was physically fit and prided herself in keeping up with those younger than herself. And being blessed with good genes, she looked half her age. She was in complete denial about the aging process until recently when her reluctance to roll out of bed seemed an unwelcome reminder that she was not quite as young as she thought she was, but not old enough to complain about it.

Not only did that rude awakening hit her like a wave of cold water, but it actually frightened her. She had always believed that aging was the younger cousin to death. If the process was starting, she feared finding herself on the slippery downhill slope of that mountain, unwillingly coasting toward her final days. With a heightened sense of her own mortality, she began a beauty and anti-aging regimen that included Oil of Olay, vitamins, healthy eating, and exercise.

For her, the whole aging process was like having an out-of-body experience where she hovered like a spectator in the atmosphere, watching gravity molest her skin, fat, and boobs. That very thought caused Grace to fall into depression, often accompanied by copious periods of weeping. She tried to dismiss the intrusive thoughts of sickness and death that often interrupted her peace of mind and tried to re-ignite her zest for life. She was determined to outrun time any way she could, be it potion or pill, hope or will.

Rubbing her bleary eyes and slowly opening them, she stretched her entire body. She was startled by a sudden crick in her neck. "Ahhh...oh, Lord!" she muttered. Her mouth opened in a silent scream, and she cautiously grabbed her neck to massage away the pain. She held her breath briefly, attempting to stifle her frequent allergy-induced sneeze that she knew would cause her bladder to splatter. The effort failed, and she sneezed six times in succession.

But Grace refused to lose her feminine allure. In an effort to intimidate Mother Nature's cruel humor, she made it a point to search for, find and invest in the kind of undergarments that would guard against incontinence and yet let her feel young and beautiful.

She smiled, inwardly at least, and dismissed the minor joint pain and body aches that she felt as she slowly sat up on the edge of the bed. As her feet sank into the blue sea of soft plush carpet, she contemplated as she did every morning what the golden secret was to affect and delay her signs of aging. She really felt like throwing a giant temper tantrum in the middle of the floor, kicking and screaming, "But I don't wanna, No! You can't make me! It's not fair!"

Grace checked herself against such petty worrying and remembered the old saying, "If you don't get old, you die young." She made a mental note to remember those words during her sure to come next moments of struggle with 'leveling up' on her next birthday. Although, she personally thought the saying was a crock.

She felt her stomach churning and regretted the previous night's dinner indulgence, which was threatening to come back up. She had an affinity for lukewarm Dasani water and grabbed the water bottle that sat on her nightstand. Believing in its restorative healing and digestive power, she opened it and drank the liquid down her throat in one gulp. "Ahhh, not entirely awful," she said, wiping her mouth with her hand. She let out a loud burp, thanks to an annoying case of GERD. Apparently, the delicious, cheesy chicken fricassee that she ate for dinner aggravated her gastrointestinal system.

Fortunately for her, the water did the job and helped to soothe her gurgling tummy. She slipped her Ugg's on and gently stretched her right leg and then the left – she felt tinges of pain and a slight stitch in her side. It was not debilitating, just irritating. She could almost hear her body saying, "You know you're old, right?" But she let it go, stood up, and made her way to the bathroom to brush her teeth and shower.

As she walked, out of nowhere, a stabbing pain attacked the big toe of her left foot. However, she was not surprised; the intermittent throbbing ailment that happened every now and then didn't last long and always disappeared until next time. Despite the pain, she managed to hobble to the bathroom, clad in her oversized thread-worn cotton t-shirt that kept the night sweats at bay. The hot flashes tamed so she could actually get a good night's sleep.

She ran water into the basin and washed her face, lips, and eyebrows. She studied her reflection in the mirror and realized aging was not for the faint at heart. Most of the time, she saw herself in the mirror, but she did not look at herself. She disrobed and took a moment to take in her full appearance. "Ugh! she gasped aloud!" The neuroses and negative feelings whispered tauntingly, "You look terrible. Why are there etched lines in your forehead?" "You have bags under your eyes." "You look stupid." "Cellulite." "Side-pockets." "Broken veins."

The consciousness of her fading beauty suddenly burst like a bank of delayed fireworks. She realized that the journey of growing older was not at all what had turned her self-esteem into an emotional roller coaster. She realized that the thoughts that assaulted her had more to do with her own self-acceptance and body image than anything else.

"Stop," she chided herself. Grace was tired of the niggling and persistent petty voices that looped in her head, telling her that she was past her prime and beyond her use-by date. Decidedly, she took on a more fearless attitude and an optimistic outlook toward what really was happening to her body. She silenced the vicious self-attacks. She reminded herself of her friends who missed the last class reunion, not because of their busy schedules but God had called them home.

Aging was an inevitable part of life - chins double, waistlines expand, hair grays, and eyelids sag. She realized that she may not be the 'hot chick' she used to be, but she was grateful to be alive.

She stepped into the shower, toes flinching as they touched the chilled ceramic floor. She looked up and felt God's presence, "Daughter, you are mine." She smiled triumphantly at her small bulge of a stomach and thanked God for His aging grace.

HIS HEART

> *"The heart of her husband doth safely trust in her, so that he shall have no need of spoil. She will do him good and not evil all the days of her life."*
>
> — PROVERBS 31:11-12

Solomon shoved his hands in his coat pockets and walked toward his car. This had undoubtedly been one of the most challenging days of his life. Management eliminated his position. He had just lost his six-figure position through no fault of his own. He had a wife, two children, looming medical bills, a mortgage to pay, daycare, school fees, and the burden of meeting the household's basic needs. He worried that his husbandly priesthood would be jeopardized due to this unfortunate circumstance.

As a Bible-believing Christian, what Solomon had to do was quite simple: remember to follow his father's example and be the priest of his home and a good provider. These duties were principles imprinted in his psyche from his father, grandfather, and uncles. They had modeled a strong, single-minded work ethic that allowed them to provide food and shelter and a secure life for their families.

Solomon and Debera had been married more than ten years. He was a prestigious VP of Marketing, and she was a successful financial executive. By all standards, they were well-off and lived comfortably in a quaint suburban neighborhood. They were extremely committed to firmly managing their lives with an eye on their economic needs. Since their union, to maintain their trust and guard their relationship's health, they shared the tasks of paying bills and building their investments. They both tithed ten percent of their incomes, planned their expenditures, watched their financial transactions, invested a portion of income, and divided 20% equally between themselves for their own personal financial needs. Their economic security was a major priority. And then life suddenly changed.

Solomon was a man of faith who always hoped for the best but wisely planned for the worst. He was known for being optimistic and upbeat, someone who appeared to keep everything in proper perspective. But today, under his calm exterior, Solomon felt a huge pit growing deep within him.

It was late afternoon as he unlocked the door of his 2018 BMW 750Li, got in, and pushed the button to adjust the seat. He leaned his head on the headrest and looked up and through the sunroof at the blue skies that could be seen through the smudges of fingerprints of his playful children.

Although it was late afternoon, the day was still in full swing. People were busily moving about, but he could see little except the cloud that hung over him at that moment. Two hours earlier, just at the end of his regular workday, his job had been terminated. He felt a gnawing shame of being in a position in which he would not adequately meet his family's needs as he should. He felt his identity as a provider was in jeopardy.

"God!" he screamed as he hit his fist on the steering wheel. His reaction was not driven by anger but rather a mixture of fear and frustration.

He drew in a deep breath as he realized he needed to take time to regroup. He immediately reminded himself to pray for God's promises, and at that moment, his car became his altar. He prayed and praised. Opening his clenched fist, he turned his palms upward, reached out to God - inviting Him to ease the tension in his mind and heart, calm his frustration, and give him the direction to lead and provide for his family.

He thanked God for being there in his hard situation and ended his prayer with the scripture, "Let my prayer be counted as incense before you, and the lifting up of my hands as the evening sacrifice." (Psalm 141:2) He pulled a kerchief from his blue suit jacket and wiped his nose. He felt some relief and trusted that the words he needed to tell Debera the news of his day would come when needed.

Solomon loved his wife very much and wanted to protect her from problems that would worry or upset her. He had loved her at first sight and was totally devoted to her. Her beauty and perfect grace amazed him. Her spirit of selflessness and kindness toward everyone she met was refreshing.

She made him want to be a better version of himself. He felt the two of them could talk about anything.

He also knew she was not a superficial woman. He knew she could be happy forever in a little house with just him, the children, her clothes, and her bible. Yet, he dreaded breaking this news to her.

His mind drifted to the first crisis they faced only five years into their marriage. He had to have cardiac bypass surgery, and he still remembered her reaction when they received the news. He had watched as she tried desperately to maintain her composure. But, he could not miss the fear in her eyes betraying her brave façade.

That day as the cardiologist explained the procedure, Solomon reached to take Debera's hand, squeezing it to reassure her that it would be alright. She responded with a gentle answering squeeze affirming with him their confident faith in God. But, post-surgery, their faith was again tested with a major complication. He had developed a heart rhythm disorder that resulted in a longer stay in the hospital and increased hospital costs.

The impact that the illness had on his wife and family was significant. This hardship challenged the promise they made on their wedding day five years earlier. Still, Debera hunkered down and firmly solidified their love in the midst of a serious storm. She spent hours by his bedside yet worked hard every day, ensuring that the children were cared for. She knew that Solomon felt the weight on his shoulders, believing that he was "a burden to his family." But to keep him from being frustrated about what they could not control, she found small ways to love and be present for him every day. She made him laugh, shared words of affirmation, and simply held his hand.

Her feminine, soft, and caring qualities denounced his deep-rooted macho cynicism. Through it all, he watched her push, stretch, work, support, and grow as she took full responsibility for picking up the slack when he could not do his part. She balanced work and home to the point that their family counted on her every single day. And he knew that was far from easy. He thought about the effects the experience had on him and how it changed their lives forever. He realized that the course of their lives had just changed again as totally and irretrievably as it had changed that day years before.

Solomon put his car in gear, turned the radio on, and slowly drove out of the parking lot, making a right onto Holloway Street and turning to the north freeway heading toward home. It proved to be the longest ride ever. Solomon struggled within himself to believe that he no longer had a job but refused to fret about it. Instead, he formulated a plan to move forward.

Arriving home, he parked the car in the driveway well after dark. He sat there momentarily thinking about how quickly his life had changed since he had left home that morning. He stared at the lights burning in the windows of their modest brick ranch-style home and whispered a praise of thanks to God for all he had been afforded. He knew Debera was still up, waiting for him to come home. It was her routine. The children were put to bed hours ago.

He opened the door and stepped over the threshold into their home. There she stood radiantly beautiful with a smiling welcome. He swept his wife up in a hug and told her as he embraced her how much he loved her. But she had felt him tense as he said it. "I love you too," she responded and then added knowingly, "What's going on?"

In a few words, he shared with her the events of his afternoon. With genuine grace and delicacy, the news did not phase her in the least. Bound together with their faith and reassurance that God was in control, they began to "run the numbers" and devise a plan through wisdom and creativity. They prayed together. Solomon ended their prayer of faith. Debera squeezed his hand to reassure him that everything would work out. He responded with a firm responsive squeeze in agreement that through God's guidance and faithfulness, they would find a way through this crisis as well.

They spent the rest of the evening laughing, talking, and enjoying each other's company. They finally made their way to their bedroom for the night. He watched as she went through her bedtime rituals and thought how blessed he was to have her at his side.

Solomon was thankful to have a wife who modeled the attributes of the Proverbs 31 woman's faith and love. Debera firmly relied on the hand of God to safeguard and strengthen their marriage even during tough times. And her love and reassurance both to Solomon and her family became evidence that God's grace was a supernatural mantle of blessing over them.

PERFECT

"Above all, love each other deeply, because love covers over a multitude of sins."

— 1 PETER 4:8

*S*he was a woman with a plan. And it had all fallen into place.

Well, not exactly; it was more like it had happened at a snail's pace. Landing the man of her dreams had taken longer than anticipated in light of her romantic failures, she finally decided to nix her "list." She decided to quit trying to force it and just accept that romance was not something she was good at.

Professional success came easy for her. She had an unbridled thirst in pursuing her career, and at times her work life was often out of balance. But her sense of personal fulfillment seemed elusive. She struggled with the push and pull between work, personal relationships, and social life.

Kennedy thought highly of herself, although others thought her to be superficial, impractical, and often bordering on absurd. The girl was abruptly real – funny, frank, and unafraid to show her strength. The flaw of her huge ego blinded her to what was obvious to everyone who encountered her. Those who knew her either really liked her or quite simply did not.

She didn't care one way or the other how other people perceived her. She was a prominent attorney and a well-respected black voice in her community, serving on several local boards. She was chic, worked hard to maintain her perfect image, and was a gung-ho fitness freak who worked out when she was not working. She was stunningly fit with a well-toned body. Her thick, long black bone-straight hair accented her radiant hazel eyes that made men love her beauty. At the same time, they deplored her aggressive, selfish, and insensitive personality.

There were certain types of men that she felt were "beneath her." She was affluent and did not want to bother with the lower class. A blue-collar boyfriend was out of the question. Her man had to be educated by way of matriculation from an accredited four-year college at a minimum. That was the way she rolled.

That is until she met *him*.

He was not at all the man she had envisaged in her dreams. With only a GED, hardhat, and Dickies jumpsuits, Ivan made his living as a construction foreman and oozed testosterone-filled manliness. He was as common as cornbread and not strikingly handsome at all.

He lived and worked as a construction foreman, was fifty years old, stood five foot nine inches tall with a slight cuddly spare tire instead of a six-pack. He sported a silver-gray and faded-pepper haircut with a receding hairline. He wore thick, black-rimmed glasses and had angry razor rash on the back of his neck.

He was quiet, not outspoken, clearly street smart, and a "bad-boy" but in a good way. He had the kind of flavor to him that made him popular among women of all ages. His relatives loved him, his friends admired him, and even some who had only heard of him respected him.

Kennedy and Ivan's love was serendipitous. He moved her emotionally, intellectually, and deep in her soul. She fought to resist him but failed. It was peculiar to her that he had no "game." He was genuine with no hidden agenda. She knew what chivalry was, but it was not something she had experienced first-hand. Not because it was dead, but because she was too busy flipping the script to prove her independence instead of receiving the courtesy and kindness of a man.

They met on a manic Monday when Kennedy's day was fully under the spell of Murphy's Law. She had missed a deadline, lost a major court case, broke the heel on her favorite Louboutin pumps, and now here she was, out of gas on the freeway with no cell phone. As she sat on the side of the road, several cars and trucks raced by. She took several deep breaths, closed her eyes, and counted off the seconds that she would wait for her knight in shining armor to rescue her...she counted quietly one, two, three...that was it. "Who am I kidding?" she said to herself, "Unh-unh ... the only man I'm waiting on is Jesus, and I'm not waiting for Him if I can do it myself!"

After her three-count, Kennedy retrieved her ballet flats from the back seat, slipped them on, and popped open her trunk – complete with all of the QVC road rescue gadgets that she would need in an emergency, including her designer gas can. She smiled at the chance to use her hot pink Lady Can – it was the only thing to brighten the experience; that is, until her immediate next thought, how far was a gas station?

She took her credit card out of her billfold, placed her purse in the trunk, and proceeded to lock the car. Mentally beating herself up for her carelessness, she backtracked in her brain as to the whereabouts of her iPhone and tried to prepare herself for the long-graveled trek to a gas station.

As she mentally rehearsed her series of mini disasters, Ivan pulled up behind her candy apple red Mercedes Benz GLC Coupe. His 1990 faded black Ford pickup truck stood out against her luxury machine. He shut the engine down and got out of the truck to offer his help.

"May I assist you?" he smiled and introduced himself, "I'm Ivan Grant." "No, thank you. I've got it handled," she frowned and peered into his eyes reluctantly with a shake of her head and began to walk around the back of her car.

"Did you just give me the stank-eye?" he laughed. "I've got sisters, I know the stank-eye when I see it!" He ignored her arrogance and continued, "You know the next gas station is six miles north of here, right?" She stopped in her tracks.

"If I can't give you a ride, at least use my cell to call for help." She half-way smiled at him, her eyes meeting his, and accepted his offer, "Why, thank you, Mr. Grant." and she called Roadside Assistance.

"May I ask your name?" Ivan said. "Kennedy Warren," she said. "Well, Kennedy, how about you put up that 'sissy' gas can you've got there and get out of the way of traffic?" they both laughed. He reached out and took hold of her wrist to lead her to the other side of the car, away from moving traffic, and surprisingly, she let him. For once in her life, she let a man lead. That was not automatic for her, not natural at all.

Kennedy was raised by a strong-willed single mother surrounded by passionate, outspoken friends with very strong personalities – she wore their traits to the tenth power. She was complicated and gave a hard time to men who were interested in her. She never let them tell her what to do or who to be, and her emotional walls were impenetrable.

But the more time she spent with Ivan, the more her heart knew he was the one, and the less she cared about her own imposed 'check-all-of-the-boxes' expectations for the perfect man. In fact, in his presence, her own shortcomings were glaring to the point that she could not help but accept them.

And now fast forward. It was two days until the wedding, and they had completed the last pre-marital counseling session. Kennedy and Ivan exited Dr. Sembole's office, and both sighed deeply in unison. They looked at one another, unsure, not knowing what to say or who should say something first.

They proceeded through the office doors to the outside lobby. Kennedy sauntered over to the cognac leather reception chair by the large Victorian windows and plopped her authentic Louis Vuitton satchel on the marble ledge. Ivan sat on the arm of the chair, stretched his legs in front of him, crossing them at the ankles, folded his arms, looked at Kennedy, and waited to listen. She turned to Ivan and said with a tinge of petulance in her voice, "Those counseling sessions were brutal."

"Yes, very telling," he said stoically with an easy agreeing nod. Unmoved by the many revelations of their sessions but concerned about Kennedy's reaction, he sensed she had more to say. Exposing the elephant in the room, he said, "So, you don't want children?" "No, I don't. I'm not a mother. That may change, but no…I've never wanted to be a mother. I don't know if you have noticed, but I'm a little selfish," she said, smiling sarcastically. "Blind Bartimaeus could see that, babe," he said jokingly. Leaning forward to take her hands between his, he rubbed them and affectionately raising them to his lips. He kissed them gently as he looked into her eyes, "But, I want my wife to carry my seed. I want to bless the world with what our love creates; a life that reflects the best of both of us, the best of our love."

His words made her melt inside, "While that is the sweetest sentiment I've ever heard, at this moment, I just can't envision it! It's just not something I want, Ivan!" At that very moment, Kennedy pulled her hands away and turned slowly to the window, gazing outward as if she was searching for another answer.

He stood, walked up behind her, draped his arms around her waist, and whispered in her ear, "Babe, it is all going to work out, I promise you, it will work out! Trust me."

Reluctant to agree, Kennedy kept her body close to his, looking back over her shoulder at him and asked, "How Ivan?" He turned her around to face him and said to her intently, "Love conquers all."

She frowned and stepped back away from him, "This isn't a Hallmark movie – love doesn't conquer all – you don't just fall in love, and everything magically works out!" He used a calm, assuring voice and responded to her, "I agree, it doesn't work out magically; it works out prayerfully. The difference in the equation, my love, is God."

Kennedy believed in God, although her family wasn't particularly religious. She resisted relinquishing control to a higher power, crosses and consecrated oil for things, preferring instead things that could be done under her own strength. Not giving in to his theory, Kennedy argued, "We are from two different worlds. I am not willing to change who I am to be what you want – if I am not who you want now, how will I be who you want with a baby?" Ivan tried to understand her concerns more than he tried to convince her, "You ARE who I want now. A baby, our baby, would represent our love in this world long after we are gone from this earth."

Kennedy had embraced her child-free identity some years ago and was not easily dissuaded. She persisted, "I don't know. I just don't know. I don't want to be forced, coerced, or guilted into something as major as becoming a parent. If we go ahead with this marriage, knowing how you feel about having a child and how I feel about not having a child, we are setting ourselves up to fail! I cannot guarantee that I will change my mind on this, Ivan."

He rested his hands on each of her shoulders, looked her directly in her almond-shaped eyes, and said, "Listen, this isn't an ultimatum. For me, it is not a deal-breaker. It is not something that has to happen right away. I love you and am totally committed to you regardless of whether we ever become parents." She heard him, but she did not believe him. "No," she said emphatically. "You want children. Why would you sacrifice your own happiness to make me happy? That is a recipe for marital discord. And that's not okay."

"So, what are you saying, Sweet?" Ivan said using the nickname he had given her. She looked at him questioningly, then dropped her eyes and tightened her lips together. She raised her head, looked at him, and shrugged her shoulders helplessly, "I don't know."

Picking up her purse from the ledge, Kennedy dug for her car keys, turned, and headed for the elevator, which arrived almost immediately. "Are you coming?" she said, looking back at her fiancé, who had followed her. "No, I'll leave you to your thoughts. In forty-eight hours though, I'll see you at the altar, yes?" Instinctively and unconsciously, he knew his bride to be. He had learned to let Kennedy work through her emotions. She talked a good game and put on a brave face. Still, she tended to overthink everything, which made her excellent at her job, but it complicated their relationship. She stopped momentarily and turned around, "Ivan, what if it doesn't work out?" He smiled, visibly confident, "What if it does?"

She half smiled with a hint of nervous composure as she stepped into the elevator. She turned, pressed the button, kissed her fingertips, and pointed them in Ivan's direction. He acknowledged her with a nod and puckered his lips to make an air kiss as the elevator doors closed. He felt elated and smiled to himself as he turned into the lobby.

Forty-eight hours passed, and their day had come. The thunder exploded loudly, and like the plunger on a pinball machine, streaks of lightning lit the gloomy gray skies sending the wedding party and its guests scurrying and bouncing about to find shelter from the storm. The luxurious sheer, white and airy voile fabrics that decorated the courtyard entrance were drenched and captured by wind gusts that blew them violently. The rain-soaked white-clad wedding party huddled together and dispersed, running two by two for shelter beneath the large, canopied tent in the courtyard. Waterlogged, limp red rose petals were strewn across the grass, and the soft, delicate sprigs of baby's breath were scattered all along the pathway. The rain poured heavily, washing noisily against the tall stained-glassed windows in the back of the chapel and hammering loudly on the roof above. Depending on the weather forecast turned out to be a worthless exercise. Every day leading up to the occasion, the summer sun shined bright, but the weather failed to cooperate on their day.

Ivan stood looking at his 5' 9" reflection in the vintage vanity tilt mirror. He adjusted his collar before buttoning his designer linen shirt that covered his angel tattooed torso. He loved his work boots and hardhat, neon shirt and safety vest included. But he was equally accustomed to dressing conservatively sharp for business and church.

He checked his watch, feeling a sense of expectation and excitement. Their wedding day put his mind into a happy state of possibilities for their future. Saying "I take this person as my own" was a powerful thing to say, and by faith, he believed their lives and future would be filled with happiness.

Ivan was only five years old when his dad abandoned his mother and sisters. He let his less-than-perfect childhood and the mistakes in prior relationships make him a better man. Hindsight had given him a clear picture of how to take care of and love a woman. The teachings and observations he made from the familial women in his life taught him the needs of a woman, the stories of their pain, their tears, what gave them joy, and what made them sad.

He held himself accountable to the word of God. As a Sunday school teacher and drummer, he took his roles seriously, and his new role as a husband would be no different. From the time he knew he wanted a wife, his prayer had been, "Lord, give me the attitude of Christ toward my future wife. Let me see her as one whom You love, and let me be Your agent for loving her."

As Ivan finished dressing, he noticed his cell phone blinking. He did not like ring tones, preferring to vibrate mode. He smiled to see that his bride had called, followed by a text message. He grabbed his jacket and headed for the door.

Kennedy refused to second guess her decision to become Mrs. Grant; after all, she only dreamed about this day, every waking moment of her life.

Ready to be united with her true love in the sight of God and their friends and family, Kennedy checked her image in the mirror for last-minute details. Wearing a gorgeous champagne tone wedding dress with a shirred bodice bearing a sweetheart neckline and a beaded lace and illusion halter. She admired her own beauty and was sure Ivan would be pleased.

Fully decked and ready to say "yes," looming in her mind was their last in-person encounter. She left their marriage counseling session knowing he wanted her to have what she wanted. But not fully sure she wanted to give him what he wanted – a baby. Having what he wanted meant Kennedy had to dig into the depths of herself to uncover that altruistic, selfless love to give the gift of a child to her future husband.

She had circled back to Dr. Sembole's office that day for individual therapy. In her soul searching, she discovered that her reluctance to have children, not surprisingly, had come from her own selfishness and her own mother's influence. Kennedy did not want the hassle, the responsibility, the worries, or to be held back. She had observed her friends with children and how they slaved, how they tired, how they grew old so much faster, how they were emotionally torn when their marriages failed, and how they were blackmailed by their exes using their own children as negotiating chips. She wanted no part of it.

She was troubled when she remembered that her mother was pregnant at seventeen, had three babies by the age of twenty-one, and two more after that. Her mom was very unhappy her whole life. She would tell Kennedy and her siblings they would be similarly unhappy if they had children. She would say to them, "Trust me, you don't want nothing you have to feed!"

In the several hours leading up to their nuptials, Kennedy learned a lot about herself, about feelings, and about communication that she had not considered. She had waffled and agonized about whether to go ahead with their marriage plans and decided that she wanted to spend her life with Ivan more than anything. He was willing to put up with her quirks. As she waited to meet her groom at the altar, her maid of honor adjusted her veil. With trembling fingers, Kennedy picked up her phone and texted her love, "I see our vows not just as promises, but as privileges. I get to laugh with you and cry with you, care for you and share with you,

M. DARLENE CARSON

I get to run with you and walk with you, I get to build with you and live with you, and I get to bless the world with what our love creates; a life that reflects the best of both of us, the best of our love. See you at the altar."

FIXED

"Then she cried out to the LORD in her trouble, and He delivered her from her distress."

— PSALM 107:6

She opened her eyes, overcome with fear. She had no clue where she was, and try as she would, she remembered nothing. She felt pain in her lower extremities, and her mind was searching for answers.

What happened to her? Dazed, confused, and left for dead, she lay on the cold asphalt, unable to pick herself up off the ground. She tried to scream for help, but her voice and words seemed to be stuck inside of her. She had a million mixed thoughts floating in her head in a matter of seconds, but they seemed muddled and confusing.

A moment of clarity suddenly filled with hope and fear. She began desperately searching for her cell phone, her arms flailing about in the fog of her confusion. "Oh crap!" she exclaimed. There was dismay and sharp disappointment in her voice when she discovered that her phone was submerged in a puddle of water. Frustrated, she beat the ground with her hands, grabbed a handful of dirt and gravel, and threw it in the air. She could not feel her legs or move them, so she lay there stuck and shivering, hoping that someone would come along and help her.

Her surroundings seemed vaguely familiar, and she tried to recall what happened to her, how she ended up in this place. Just for a moment, she paused, looking up at the moon shining on the backdrop of a steel-gray sky, and began praying that her strength would be greater than the fear she was feeling. She pleaded with God to rescue her, cautiously and intentionally refraining from offering anything in exchange for His Divine assistance.

Inid was a certified wild child, a legitimate earth disturber. When sin crouched at her door, she welcomed it like an old friend and entertained it like a playful cousin. She was sure that somewhere along the glorious corridors of Heaven, her photo was posted up like America's Most Wanted. She had stacked broken promises to God like parking violations; and, with a cavalier attitude, treated them as minor offenses. Her promises were empty. They were mere words to placate or stall until she got what she wanted.

The close encounters in her life's journey would make chief sinners blush. She acted impulsively and took unwise risks for pleasure and entertainment only. Her choices resulted in stupid mistakes that created some very serious consequences in her life and the lives of those connected to her.

In fact, her reckless behavior had earned her the nickname Kat from her Nana, who declared Inid had more lives than a cat because of her near and not-so-near brushes with death. She warned her granddaughter of her potentially fatal actions. She predicted that she would 'bust hell wide open' for being 'fast and frisky.' She would kiss Nana's forehead laughingly, adding, "I'll be alright as long as you're praying, Nana."

Nana would chide back with stern sincerity, "Prayer don't fix what don't want to be fixed, baby."

None of Nana's admonitions pricked her conscience, and Inid had continued down a path of distraction and destruction until now. She scolded herself for being so careless with her life, for the shamelessness she allowed to consume her. She continued to lay there on the cold pavement, dejected and reviewing her past. She couldn't help but think that her present situation was partially brought on by her past behaviors.

As her outer senses began to fade, from deep within all her hopes and dreams, missed opportunities, unkept promises, the faces of dear loved ones, and her favorite memories played out like images looping over and over again in her mind. She began to spiral down as a wave of heavy, haunting thoughts drove her into a place of darkness and regrets.

She recognized the faces of those she had wronged, felt the impact of the disappointment that she had caused others, and saw the open wounds of hurt that her passion for petty and mean-spirited folly had spun. She was taunted by the voices of guilt as she tried to focus, fighting the fog in her brain that seemed to be draining her physical strength.

Tears poured from her eyes, and as groggy and confused as she was, Inid sensed a long-suppressed need to be spiritually healed. She realized she had always chosen the wrong path, and it was time to change direction. She felt as if she was fading fast, and her proverbial "come to Jesus" moment had arrived.

She scanned the now blue-black sky left and right, shaking her head mournfully as she mumbled, "please forgive me." The words rolled from her lips repeatedly. She was genuinely sorry, not for herself but for the trouble she had caused. Suddenly she saw a dazzlingly pure, bright, white shining light that broke into her darkened soul and lifted her up. She felt as if she was floating in space, and she did not want to come down. For the first time in a while, she was at peace.

WEIGHT ON THE LORD

"Do you not know that your bodies are temples of the Holy Spirit, who is in you, whom you have received from God? You are not your own; you were bought at a price. Therefore, honor God with your bodies."

— I CORINTHIANS 6:19-20

God will give you strength and the desires of your heart. I am a witness!

I was at a place that was all too familiar in my life: lonely and confused about the direction my life would take because of all the wrong turns I had already taken. My emotional state contributed to low self-esteem and a negative attitude. I remember feeling like I was at rock bottom, desperate for a change. I fell to my knees that day, repenting and accepting Christ into my mess of a life!

When I started the amazing new journey as a Believer, I wanted Christ more than I wanted anything! More than I wanted all the vices and voices that had separated me from Him. My love for Him had finally exceeded my love of the sins and transgressions that keeps us all on countless family prayer lists!

I made a choice, and with the help of the Holy Spirit, I quit everything instantly and never looked back! No triggers. No temptations. No fallbacks. I boldly lived my new and holy life, declaring my testimony and letting my example be a living message for Christ!

And just as my faith and my relationship with Christ grew, my spiritual knowledge deepened as well. In the name of Jesus, my life was fully new.

But I noticed something else. My waist was growing, too. My fearfully and wonderfully made body was swelling into a barely recognizable me!

My new life as a Spirit-filled believer was filled with a whole lot of churchin', which unfortunately included a whole lot of eating! My joy in the Lord had become filled with conferences, anniversary dinners, revivals, buffets, prayer meetings, fellowship potlucks, street ministry, fish fries, concerts, chicken dinners, retreats, and bake sales. And, other than a few victory laps around the church, my lifestyle became mostly sedentary.

I struggled to even fast. A few days without food? Where they do that at? Turn my plate down? I found myself asking God, "Turn down for what?" I honestly found it to be a serious struggle to deny myself the utter deliciousness of certain delicacies. I mean, there are some things that you just don't say no to, namely – my mom Gerri's pound cake, my daughter Gigi's rolls, and Krispy Kreme doughnuts.

Ironically, I had been able to walk away from every narcotic addiction that was destroying my life. But, I refused to release my love for deep-fried anything, pasta everything, and chocolate whatever! Even for the God who gave His only begotten Son to die for me so that I could live. Dang, that's disrespectful and downright embarrassing!

But was I really living? Or was I failing to embrace this life of mercy that I was blessed to receive by dying from what was meant to give me sustenance? Food.

Despite my doctors' warnings to lose weight, reduce intake, and exercise. I continued down an unhealthy path knowing full well a change was needed for my temple's sake unless I wanted to meet Jesus sooner rather than later.

I know that having the testimony 'he brought me from a mighty long way' does not mean transforming me from rank sinner to sanctified glutton! That is a sin in itself!

So here she is, the elder, quoting scriptures "let the weak say I am strong" and "let the poor say, I am rich" while fat-shaming myself by adding "let the fat say I am skinny!"

Well, you can say it, pray it, quote it, or write it. Still, you can't eat yourself into oblivion and expect God to suck the fat right out of you. They can't slay fat in the healing line, no matter how anointed the preacher is! Ironically enough, the weight gain has pushed me to the prayer line because of all of the unhealthiness resulting from it!

As comfortable as I claimed to be in my own body, my truth is that the wavering reflection of the person I used to be vanished, and I struggle to bring her back at all. So, I refuse to look in mirrors. If anyone points a camera at me, I'm running and ducking like celebrities avoiding the paparazzi, reluctant to let pictures be taken or posted of me, and unwilling to face the harsh truth that those photos tell. My children refuse to take those quick, spontaneous selfies with me because it ends up being twenty takes and an endless photo-snapping session with me scrutinizing my flaws, analyzing my imperfections, and criticizing my faults.

To be clear, this has less to do with society's set of beauty standards and more to do with my own personal self-acceptance. I admire women who accept their full-figured body image. They are my "sheroes." They talk about being big and beautiful with all confidence, and I have tried to follow suit with them but cannot feel good about my body or size.

No. I don't want to deprive myself of culinary pleasures, but this girlie-girl had to face it. I had to change my whole eating lifestyle, and it is undoubtedly the hardest thing I have ever had to do.

The struggle is real. And in my transparency, I am becoming aware that I can enjoy the comfort of living in Christ's grace, even when I am uncomfortable with my own performance, choices, and insufficiencies. While in my flesh I may be tempted to ask for some kind of overnight miracle, I realize that He is miraculously able to make me strong and to fight this battle in His power, not my own.

So, I have decided to love myself enough to say "yes" to healthier choices and "no" to hypertension, diabetes, flabby arms, and bat wings.

As I continue this journey of loving and taking care of my temple more, I am so thankful that in the eyes of my Creator, no matter how much cellulite I have or how many inches I pinch, He has confirmed through his word that "I am fearfully and wonderfully made."

I may not ever be perfect, but I can forever be perfectly His.

AFTERWORD

What is your story? Whatever it is, don't let your past, circumstances, environment, or perceived insufficiency define your worth.

Celebrate the "SHE" that God has created you to be, realizing and appreciating the gift you are to those around you. Renew your mind and align yourself with the word of God as He molds you with the unique characteristics that make you the powerful Proverbs 31 woman that you were created to be.

AFTERWORD

31 CHARACTERISTICS OF A PROVERBS 31 WOMAN

1. A Proverbs 31 Woman is noble. Proverbs 31:10
2. A Proverbs 31 Woman is trustworthy. Proverbs 31:11
3. A Proverbs 31 Woman honors husband. Proverbs 31:12
4. A Proverbs 31 Woman is hardworking. Proverbs 31:13
5. A Proverbs 31 Woman is selective. Proverbs 31:14
6. A Proverbs 31 Woman makes wise choices. Proverbs 31:14
7. A Proverbs 31 Woman always has a plan. Proverbs 31:15
8. A Proverbs 31 Woman uses money wisely. Proverbs 31:16
9. A Proverbs 31 Woman works willingly. Proverbs 31:17
10. A Proverbs 31 Woman supports her family. Proverbs 31:18
11. A Proverbs 31 Woman works hard. Proverbs 31:19
12. A Proverbs 31 Woman is generous. Proverbs 31:20
13. A Proverbs 31 Woman sees the big picture. Proverbs 31:21

AFTERWORD

14. A Proverbs 31 Woman is creative. Proverbs 31:22
15. A Proverbs 31 Woman honors her family. Proverbs 31:23
16. A Proverbs 31 Woman is talented. Proverbs 31:24
17. A Proverbs 31 Woman is future prepared. Proverbs 31:25
18. A Proverbs 31 Woman is wise. Proverbs 31:26
19. A Proverbs 31 Woman speaks kindly. Proverbs 31:26
20. A Proverbs 31 Woman is watchful/busy. Proverbs 31:27
21. A Proverbs 31 Woman fears the Lord. Proverbs 31:30
22. A Proverbs 31 Woman receives praise. Proverbs 31:31
23. A Proverbs 31 Woman good deed rewards. Proverbs 31:31
24. A Proverbs 31 Woman defends defenseless. Proverbs 31:8
25. A Proverbs 31 Woman wishes no one bad. Proverbs 31:3
26. A Proverbs 31 Woman has high standards. Proverbs 31:22
27. A Proverbs 31 Woman hopeful for future. Proverbs 31:25

AFTERWORD

28. A Proverbs 31 Woman blesses others. Proverbs 31:28
29. A Proverbs 31 Woman worth more than jewels. Proverbs 31:10
30. A Proverbs 31 Woman trusted of everyone. Proverbs 31:11
31. A Proverbs 31 Woman does good, no harm. Proverbs 31:12

ABOUT THE AUTHOR

M. Darlene Carson is a C-Suite Executive Assistant by profession but when she is not scheduling a gazillion meetings for a non-profit CEO or transcribing minutes, she is creating. Founder of Words to Life Drama Ministry LLC and DollHouse Inspirations, she is a playwright, producer, poetess with a vision to create works of integrity. With the pen of a 'ready writer', she uses her talent to inspire the lives of those who seek greater spiritual meaning and a deeper relationship with Christ.

Founder of Words to Life Drama Ministry (WTLDM) and DollHouse Inspirations (DHI), she is a passionate writer with a vision to create written works of integrity. She produces her own writing via the WTLDM production company and writes plays, monologues, poetry, creates spiritual greeting cards through DollHouse Inspirations, and writes a blog "Her Pen".

A member of the Dramatist Guild of America and the International Centre for Women Playwrights, she has penned, produced, and directed several stage and musical productions which explore Christian themes, faith, and values.

Some of her production work includes: "Those Sorry Saint's", "Saints & Ain'ts", Ain't No Half-Step'n", "The Promise", "The Three Pigs", "Preacher, Preacher", "A Wing and A Prayer", "The Man Store", "Counterfeit Christmas", "Love Knots", "That's Life", "SHE", "Cross", and she is presently working to produce a Holy Hip Hopera entitled "Street Lights".

Darlene is a native of Beckley, WV, who now resides in Columbus, OH. She is an ordained elder who comes alive when she can use her experience as a women's ministry leader to promote unity and sisterhood through a solid relationship with Christ.

Longtime resident of Columbus, Ohio, she is married to Darrell Carson and has five daughters, one son, fourteen (14) grandchildren, and one great grandchild.

facebook.com/darlene.carson.9

twitter.com/wrds2life

instagram.com/wrds2life